SUMMARY

Where the

Crawdads Sings

Book by

Delia Owens

Epic-Summary

TABLE OF CONTENTS

INTRODUCTION

The novel's main narrative opens in the marshland near the fictional town of Barkley Cove, North Carolina. Seven-year-old Catherine "Kya" Clark lives in a shack in the swamp with her mother, father, and siblings. However, one day, Kya's mother leaves the shack forever in order to escape the physical abuse inflicted by Kya's father. Kya's siblings soon leave on their own as well, leaving only Kya and Pa. Pa spends increasingly more time away from the shack over the years, and when Kya is about ten years old, Pa leaves forever. Kya has become thoroughly self-sufficient by this time, living off of the land and occasionally trading in town for necessary supplies.

When Kya is 14 years old, a kind local boy named Tate Walker begins to visit Kya, and he teaches her how to read. He is about four years older than Kya. He also gives Kya his old textbooks from school. When Kya is 15 years old, she and Tate fall in love, but Tate insists that they do not have sex until Kya is older. Tate soon leaves for college, and although he promises to love and remember Kya, Kya feels abandoned. When Kya is 19 years old, she suddenly becomes attracted to a young local man named Chase Andrews. Chase begins visiting her often. Chase says that he loves her and is eager to have sex with her. Kya refuses at first, but after about a year, she consents to sex.

Tate eventually returns to Barkley Cove in order to perform scientific research on the marshland. He visits Kya and asks for forgiveness, but she refuses to take him back. Tate sees that Kya has performed much of her own research on the marshland, and he urges Kya to submit it to publishers. Tate also warns Kya that Chase is a dishonest womanizer. One day, Kya sees in the newspaper that Chase has become engaged to someone else. She is heartbroken. Later, she submits her research to publishers, and when she is 22 years old, a book of her research is published under her name. Kya's brother Jodie sees the book in a store and returns to the swamp to reconnect with Kya. Jodie encourages Kya to give Tate another chance.

Chase eventually visits Kya and says that he wants to continue his relationship with her, despite the fact that he is married to someone else. When Kya refuses him, Chase tries to rape her. She hits him and escapes. Kya realizes that because Chase is such a popular member of the town, and because she is an outcast for living in the swamp, she has no recourse. One day, in October of 1969, Chase's body is found near the swamp. He appears to have fallen—or possibly have been pushed—out of a fire watchtower. The sheriff investigates and arrests Kya. However, the evidence is inconclusive and circumstantial, and Kya is acquitted. She and Tate declare their love for each other, and they live together in the swamp. Kya continues her career as a naturalist, and Tate continues his career as a researcher. Kya dies at age 64, after which Tate finds evidence that seems to prove that Kya killed Chase. He disposes of the evidence so that no one will ever find it.

CHAPTER 1-5

The prologue opens near the town of Barkley Cove, North Carolina. It is October 30, 1969, and the recently deceased body of a man named Chase Andrews is on the ground near the marsh. Chapter 1 opens in August of 1952. Catherine "Kya" Clark, the protagonist, is six years old and lives in a shack in the marsh with her parents and her four older siblings. One day, Kya's mother leaves the shack, never to return. No one in the family speaks of Ma's departure, but Kya spends each day on the steps, waiting for Ma to return. Her older brother, Jodie, helps distract her by playing with her. In Chapter 2, over the next few weeks, Kya's siblings all leave the house to live on their own. Kya knows that they are leaving because they do not wish to live with Pa. Kya wonders why none of them took her with them. Pa, a veteran of World War Two, begins to leave the house for days at a time. On those days, Kya takes care of herself by cooking food from the garden and walking to Barkley Cove to buy food. One day, in town, she sees a boy named Chase Andrews. Soon, Kya's seventh birthday arrives.

Chapter 3 takes place in 1969. Some local boys accidentally find the body of Chase Andrews, and they go to tell the local sheriff, Ed Jackson. Sheriff Jackson, inspecting the scene, notes that Chase apparently fell to his death from the local fire tower. Also, strangely, there appear to be no footprints other than the ones left by the boys who found the body. In Chapter 4, it's autumn of 1952, and Kya is mostly living by herself. One day, a truant officer arrives at the shack and takes Kya to school. Kya has never been to school before. At school, the other kids ridicule her because she lives in the swamp. Kya decides never to return to school, and she hides whenever truant officers or other officials arrive at the house in the following days.

Chapter 5 takes place in 1969. Sheriff Jackson discusses the crime with his deputy, Joe Purdue. Chase had been a star ⬚uarterback in high school, and as an adult, he was a womanizer. Jackson and Purdue wonder if Chase's womanizing had anything to do with his death. They do not rule out the fact that Chase's death may have been accidental.

CHAPTER 6-10

Chapter 6 takes place in 1952. Kya takes out Pa's motorboat for an exploratory ride through the marsh. She encounters a boy who recognizes her as Jodie's sister. The boy looks to be about 10 or 11 years old. Kya has become lost, and the boy, Tate Walker, helps guide her home. Tate then returns home to his father, a widowed, poetry-loving fisherman whom everyone calls Scupper. Tate mentions that he has been enjoying studying biology in school. Scupper reads some poetry to Tate, and Tate finds himself thinking about his encounter with Kya earlier that day.

The original foundational element of Kya's narrative seems to be a state of abandonment and independence, as the departure of her family members fosters a state of solitude and necessary self-reliance from an early age. At this point in the novel, the narrative remains somewhat cryptic about the reasons for the family members' departures. However, there is just enough detail to allow readers to make inferences. First, Ma departs, and then each of Kya's siblings depart. At one point, the narration states that Kya "knew Pa was the reason they all left." Pa is not yet shown to be directly abusive, but the reader may infer that Pa has been physically and/or mentally abusive towards his family. That previous line of narration is then followed with this line "...what she wondered was why no one took her with them." Kya is eventually left completely alone in the shack in the swamp, and thus she must quickly adapt to a life by herself. Out of necessity, Kya teaches herself how to cook, manage the garden, and go to town for supplies. Throughout the novel, this state of self-reliance and independence dominates Kya's life and outlook.

Kya's sense of solitude and self-reliance is further engendered by her feeling of alienation from surrounding society, as the episode involving her day at school demonstrates the prejudice she faces due to the circumstances of her birth. Kya goes to school for one day because a truant officer arrives to bring her to school. However, Kya finds the lessons and activities strange, and she experiences ridicule and humiliation from the other students. The students specifically taunt Kya because she lives in the marsh. The children chant things like, "Where ya been, marsh hen? Where's yo' hat, swamp rat?"

For these reasons, Kya decides never to return to school, and she forms an even deeper bond and sense of self-identification with the marsh. Thus, between Kya's abandonment by her family and her alienation from the surrounding society, Kya becomes directly bonded to the marsh and the swamp. The only contrasting element is Kya's interaction with Tate Walker. Tate does not seem to hold prejudice against Kya, and he is even kind and helpful towards her. In this way, the novel foreshadows the bond that develops between them throughout the narrative.

Meanwhile, the novel begins building a parallel narrative that seems to have only a few connections to the main narrative, but these connections and the general air of mystery create an air of suspense and curiosity that help to propel the reader and keep them alert. While the main narrative proceeds in a linear fashion beginning in 1952, the parallel narrative begins in 1969 after the body of Chase Andrews is found. By the end of the novel's first few chapters, there are only two connections between these narratives: one location and one character. Chase Andrews makes a brief appearance as a boy in Chapter 2, and his body is found 17 years later near the marsh where Kya lives.

These connections may lead the reader to suspect that Kya may have been involved in Chase's death, but all details relating to a possible motive are obscured from both the reader and the sheriff. Joe Purdue mentions that Chase was a womanizer: "Tom-cattin', ruttin' 'round like a penned bull let out." Thus the reader may try to begin solving the mystery, but the lack of facts and evidence leaves the reader in a state of suspense.

Chapter 7 takes place in 1952. Kya, in the shack, thinks about Tate and about her increasing solitude. Pa eventually returns, and Kya makes a meal for him. The next morning, Pa and Kya get in Pa's boat to go fishing. They go fishing almost every day, and Kya hopes to encounter Tate again. One day, Pa says that his family used to be wealthy and live in Asheville. Chapter 8 takes place in 1969. Sheriff Jackson informs Chase's parents and Chase's wife Pearl of Chase's death. One day, Jackson overhears two locals gossiping and saying that Chase could have been killed by "that woman lives out in the marsh," but Jackson pays the gossip no mind. Chapter 9 takes place in 1953. Pa and Kya go to the Gas and Bait store, owned by a black man whom everyone calls Jumpin'. Pa and Kya eat in a restaurant. A woman tells her daughter not to go near Kya. Later, Pa disappears again for a few days. Kya thinks about the times that Pa, drunk, beat Kya, her siblings, and Ma. Pa eventually returns and finds a blue letter sent by mail. Kya thinks it is from Ma, and to Kya's dismay, Pa burns it before leaving again.

Chapter 10 takes place in 1969. Jackson and Purdue go to investigate the crime scene again but find nothing. They wonder if tidewater may have cleared the sand of footprints and other possible evidence.

CHAPTER 11-15

Chapter 11 takes place in 1956. Kya is ten years old, and Pa has been spending more and more time away from the shack. The supply of cash in the shack starts to run out, so Kya digs up mussels from the sand and sells them to Jumpin'. In Chapter 12, Kya continues to live on her own. She sometimes sees Tate, but she always watches him from afar rather than speaking to him. One day, she sees a group of children joyfully playing. Among them is Chase Andrews. Kya eventually begins fishing as well so that she can trade the fish in town for supplies. Jumpin' helps her arrange trades.

Chapter 13 takes place in 1960. Kya is 14 years old and living alone in the shack. She begins collecting interesting specimens from the marsh, such as bird feathers. One day, a group of boys sees her, and they all ridicule her and call her feral. She runs away. Chapter 14 takes place in 1969. A lab report confirms that Chase died from falling. The lab examination also finds strange red fibers on his jacket. Chapter 15 takes place in 1960. Kya goes looking for feathers in the marsh again, and she is surprised to see a feather placed on a stump for her, along with a milk carton containing some useful supplies. One day, she stands by the stump and sees Tate approach. She thanks him for the gift, and he offers to teach her to read.

CHAPTER 16-20

In Chapter 16, Tate teaches Kya to read, and the narration briefly exposits upon the economic decline faced by Kya's parents during the Great Depression.

The novel further develops and emphasizes Kya's sense of alienation by demonstrating how antipathy causes people in town drive Kya to further retreat into the seeming safety of her habitual environment in the swamp. As Kya continues to become more independent, she continues to develop a stronger connection with the swamp. Additionally, Kya's sense of home in the swamp continues to frame her as an object of fear and ridicule in the eyes of the townspeople. For example, when Kya and Pa eat at a restaurant, a woman in the restaurant says to her daughter, "Don't go near that girl, ya hear me? She's dirty."

The woman's antipathy and aversion towards Kya seems to be based not strictly in the belief that Kya is literally dirty, but more saliently in the belief that Kya is strange and corrupted because she has such a different background. Kya's origins and life are so strange and unfamiliar to the townspeople that the townspeople react with distrust, antipathy, and aversion. This idea is further emphasized when a group of boys encounters Kya in the woods and call her names like "Marsh Girl" and "Miss Missin' Link." This sense of fear and hatred may also contribute to the townspeople's immediate suspicion of Kya when Chase Andrews is found dead.

Kya's alienation becomes even more entrenched as she becomes increasingly alienated from her family and from her family history, as Kya's identity becomes increasingly reliant not on family connections or stories, but more on her present circumstances of survival and self-reliance. Kya learns a little about her family history when, one day, Pa suddenly says to her, "My folks weren't always po', ya know." He then provides some broad details about the former wealth of his family. Exposition in Chapter 16 provides further context for this wealth and decline, demonstrating Pa and Ma's personal economic decline during the Great Depression.

However, because Kya's family members all eventually leave her, Kya has no persistent connection to her family or her family history. Pa's destruction of the mysterious blue letter seems to be a strike against a possible reformation of a family connection. Pa then deserts Kya permanently, and her familial alienation becomes complete. This familial alienation seems to be a final step in Kya's decline into complete isolation, as she becomes a person almost entirely devoid of societal connection.

However, Kya's isolation is contrasted by two remaining societal connections—Tate and Jumpin'—and the benefits and fulfillment that Kya receives from these connections demonstrate the indelible necessity of interpersonal connection. Firstly, Kya's connection with Jumpin' is beneficial not only in a practical capacity, but also in an emotional capacity. Jumpin' is shown to be kind, thoughtful, and helpful towards Kya, simply out of the goodness of his heart. He is sympathetic towards her, and his practical support towards her seems to be symptomatic of emotional support, kindness, and sympathy as well.

Tate represents another positive connection to the outside world. He is also kind towards her and holds no prejudices. He teaches her how to read, and he is never impatient, unkind, or mocking towards her. As the narration states, "He didn't want to shame her," as he did not want to be unkind or make her uncomfortable. Through these character connections, the narrative demonstrates the emotional and practical necessities of having of positive interpersonal connections in one's life.

Chapter 17 takes place in 1960. Kya goes to Jumpin's store, and Jumpin' says that people from Social Services have been asking around town about Kya. Jumpin' lied to the officials and said that Kya's father was still living with her. Kya tells Tate this news, and he says he knows of an abandoned cabin in the marsh where Kya can hide for a while. Over the summer, Tate continues to teach Kya how to read. Tate eventually begins teaching Kya poetry, and Kya enjoys poetry very much. Tate begins his senior year at high school and brings his old textbooks for Kya to read. Kya reads them with delight and curiosity.

One day, Kya begins suffering from stomach cramps, and Tate tells her that she is having her period. It is Kya's first period, and she goes to Jumpin's wife Mabel for help. One day, when Tate is visiting Kya at the cabin, Kya and

Tate suddenly kiss. They decide to be boyfriend and girlfriend.

Chapter 18 takes place in 1960. Tate continues to visit Kya to give her lessons in various subjects, such as math. On Kya's 15th birthday, Tate brings her a birthday cake and presents. One day, in the winter, Tate's father says to Tate that he knows that Tate has been visiting Kya in the swamp. He warns Tate against impregnating Kya. Tate indignantly informs his father that he and Kya have never had sex. One day, in the spring, Kya tries to initiate sex with Tate. However, he refuses on the grounds that Kya is only 15 years old. Tate professes his love for Kya. In May, Tate informs Kya that he will be attending college in Chapel Hill, North Carolina to study biology. He says that he will visit her often. He says that he will never forget her and will never stop loving her.

Chapter 19 takes place in 1969. Patti Love, Chase's mother contacts the sheriff's office and says that she has something that may be useful to the investigation into Chase's death. Chapter 20 takes place in July of 1961. Tate has already left to work in Chapel Hill before college. Although Kya has been abandoned before, she seems to be especially heartbroken by Tate's departure. In the shack, she screams and cries and seems to fear that Tate will not return to her.

CHAPTER 21-25

Chapter 21 takes place in 1961. Still in a state of sadness, Kya begins to wonder if something about her drives people away. Kya becomes even more reclusive and goes into town as little as possible. She begins to feel very lonely. She spends her time collecting specimens of nature from the swamp. Chapter 22, takes place in 1965. Kya is 19 years old and still living alone in the swamp. She sees Chase Andrews one day and feels a faint physical attraction towards him. Meanwhile, at college, Tate has become consumed with study and research, and he feels that he should no longer visit Kya because she is from such a different world.

Kya's romantic and sexual awakenings add a layer of complication and external dependence to her existence, as she becomes dependent on the outside world not only for occasional supplies and companionship, but also for potential nourishment of her newfound sexual and romantic drives. Kya's newfound self-identification as a woman is the largest fundamental change in her self-perception since her family abandoned her. She not only undergoes the biological transformation of having her first period, but she also undergoes the transformation of developing a drive towards romance and sexual desire, both specifically aimed towards Tate.

These drives are nurtured by Tate's reciprocal love and sexual desire. Tate even says to Kya, "I love you."

However, the fulfillment of these attractions seems to ultimately be stymied by considerations of age and social separation. Kya wishes to have sex with Tate, but Tate refuses due to the fact that Kya is only 15 years old. Moreover, the persistence of their loving relationship is disrupted due to Tate's relocation to Chapel Hill for college. Thus, while Kya's sexual and romantic awakenings seem to add a greater drive towards connection with others, they also seem to create a greater capacity for disappointment.

The profundity and significance of Tate's departure mark a deepening of Kya's reclusion from society, as Tate's departure thematically echoes the departure of Kya's family, and the subsequent pain seems to drive Kya towards further reclusion. Although Kya seemed to suffer feelings of sadness and fear following her family's abandonment of her, her pain following Tate's departure seems to be much more intense. She returns to the shack, where she screams and cries. This outpouring of emotion seems to be symptomatic of a deep sense of pain and betrayal; Kya had grown to love Tate deeply, and thus his departure marks an intense tragedy and disappointment for Kya.

The departure drives Kya into further reclusion. As the narration states, "For a month…Kya did not leave her place, did not go into the marsh or to Jumpin's for gas or supplies." Kya then went into town as little as possible and continued to live in a state of near total isolation for years. These facts mark a deepening of Kya's isolation, as the pain of Tate's perceived betrayal seems to have further alienated

Kya from the hope of having a fulfilling interpersonal connection.

When Chapter 22 foreshadows a possible interpersonal connection between Kya and Chase, the narrative seems to emphasize the fact that Kya's attraction towards Chase is of a desperate and physical quality, thus far removed from the romance and fulfillment that seemed to be promised by Kya's relationship with Tate. When Kya watches him from afar, the narration states, "her body watched Chase Andrews, not her heart." Thus, Kya's possible attraction towards Chase appears to be merely physical rather than emotional or romantic.

However, and underlying emotional element may be inferred by the reader in that Kya's years of isolation may have compounded her desire for some type of interpersonal connection. Thus, although Kya has developed into a potentially embittered, lonely young woman, she may be developing an attraction towards Chase due to an instinctual drive towards romantic and/or sexual companionship.

Chapter 23 takes place in 1965. One day, Kya encounters Chase in the marsh. They spend the rest of the day together and even kiss. Chase tries to initiate sex. He is aggressive. Kya hits him and runs away. In Chapter 24, Chase visits Kya at her shack the next day and apologizes for his actions. Kya forgives him, and they go to the nearby fire tower to look at the marsh from above. Kya gives Chase a shell necklace that she made. They then go to Kya's shack, and Chase is impressed with the many specimens that Kya has found and labeled.

Chase says that he is fascinated by Kya and likes her very much. Kya feels a stir of hope for love. Chapter 25 takes place in 1969. Patti Love, Chase's mother, visits the sheriff's office. She says that Chase always wore a shell necklace that was supposedly a present from   Kya, but the necklace was not on his body when his body was found. Patti says that the sheriff should investigate Kya.

CHAPTER 26-30

Chapter 26 takes place in 1965. Chase begins visiting Kya regularly. They spend time together in the marsh, never in town. They kiss but do not have sex. Tate has graduated from college and is now in graduate school. He has planned to focus his research on marshland ecology. He has also realized that he loves Kya and wants to marry her. However, when he visits her, he sees her with Chase and leaves. Using library books, Kya has become very knowledgeable about biology, ecology, and zoology. Chase says that he is falling in love with Kya and wants to have sex with her, but Kya does not wish to have sex. She asks when Chase will introduce her to his friends and parents, and he says that he will soon.

Chapter 27 takes place in 1966. Kya and Chase have been together for about a year. Chase suggests that they build a place of their own on the outskirts of town. He suggests that she come with him on a trip to Asheville. In Asheville, they stay in a motel. Chase says that they should have sex, and Kya agrees, but she finds the sex unsatisfying. Afterwards, Kya asks when Chase will he will start incorporating her into the rest of his life. He says that it is somewhat complicated, but he will soon. A few months later, Tate visits Kya's shack to ask for forgiveness. He also says that Chase is going out with other women in town.

Kya, angry at Tate, tells him to go away. Tate advises Kya to send her collected samples to a publisher for money.

Chapter 28 takes place in 1969. Sheriff Jackson talks to a fisherman who says that he saw Kya on her boat heading towards the fire tower on the night of Chase's death. Chapter 29 takes place in 1967. Chase continues to visit Kya. They have sex, but the sex is never satisfying for Kya. One day, Kya sees in the newspaper that Chase has become engaged to marry a woman named Pearl.

Kya's growing love for Chase marks a resurgence of hope for a connection with the outside world, demonstrating the fact that Kya's underlying desire to connect with society is innate and cannot be destroyed by disappointment or abandonment. Kya has suffered many crushing abandonments in her life, from her parents to her siblings to Tate. However, as she becomes increasingly attracted to Tate, she develops a renewed hope not just for love, but also for a chance to incorporate herself into life beyond the marsh. The narration states that with Chase, Kya begins to feel "The first hope in her heart since Tate left."

Kya apparently cannot rid herself of the innate human desire for connection, and Chase's attention seems to have reawakened that desire in her. Moreover, Chase's attention seems to promise the idea that Chase will help to incorporate Kya into town life. As the narration states, "Kya started to picture him taking her on a picnic with his friends. All of them laughing, running into the waves." Kya is excited by the prospect of finally being accepted by outside society with Chase's help. Chase fuels Kya's hopes by saying that he does plan on introducing her to his friends and family at some point.

However, as the narrative continues, Chase's true nature of inconsideration, manipulation, and selfishness becomes increasingly apparent, thereby foreshadowing yet another instance of betrayal and pain for Kya. Chase repeatedly promises that he will introduce Kya to his friends and parents, but he takes no actual steps towards doing so. Moreover, the reader has already been alerted in Chapter 5 to the fact that Chase is a womanizer. Further evidence of Chase's dishonest ways is presented in Chapter 27 when Tate says to Kya, "You don't live in town. You don't know that Chase goes out with other women. Just the other night I watched him drive away after a party with a blonde in his pickup. He's not good enough for you."

The reader may infer that Tate is possibly lying so that Kya will break up with Chase. However, Tate has not been shown to be deceptive or dishonest in the past, apart from his abandonment of Kya. Regardless, when Kya sees the article about Chase's engagement, Tate's accusations against Chase prove to be true. Thus these elements of foreshadowing are important for building to the revelation and to Kya's consequent feelings of pain and betrayal.

The continued development of Tate's storyline bears a mixture of hope and tragedy, for although Tate personally recommits to his love for Kya, his abandonment of Kya may have permanently damaged the healthy, loving relationship that they had formed previously. While in college, Tate became convinced that his and Kya's lives were too different for them to be together. However, he eventually realized that he could not stop loving Kya and that he wanted to be with her forever. Unfortunately, the pain of his abandonment still deeply affects Kya.

When he finally visits her again to ask for forgiveness. Kya yells at him in a fury. Tate then admits, "You're right about me, Kya. Everything you said is true…I'll never bother you again. I just need to apologize and explain." Thus, it seems that the emotional damage of Tate's betrayal may be indelible. However, the possibility of eventual reconciliation between them remains a faint but persistent source of narrative hope.

Chapter 30 takes place in 1967. Kya is extremely upset following the revelation of Chase's marriage. She realizes that she has been used and manipulated. She calms herself slightly by reciting poetry by Amanda Hamilton, a poet.

CHAPTER 31-35

Chapter 31 takes place in 1968. Kya is now 22 years old. A book written by her—The Sea Shells of the Eastern Seaboard—is scheduled to be published soon, and she looks forward to writing more books. She has become highly knowledgeable in her field due to her self-teaching. Kya gives a copy to Jumpin' and also sends a copy to Tate. Kya learns that her family owns the marsh, and she plans to pay the back taxes on it with the money from her books. Tate visits Kya one day to tell her that he read her book and that it is great.

Chapter 32 takes place in 1969. Sheriff Jackson learns that, on the night of Chase's death, Kya was in Greenville to meet with her publisher. This seems like a strange coincidence to Jackson. Moreover, the bus schedules show that she could have taken a bus back in the night and then returned to Greenville before daytime, so Jackson decides to re□uest a warrant to search Kya's home.

Chapter 33 takes place in 1968. Jodie suddenly arrives at the shack. He is a war veteran and is now attending college. He saw Kya's book in a store and decided that he needed to visit her. He asks for forgiveness for abandoning her, and Kya forgives him. Kya recalls physical abuse that Pa inflicted on his wife and children. Jodie says that he does not know where any of the other family members are except for Ma, who died two years ago of leukemia. Kya is deeply saddened by the news. Kya and

Jodie talk about their lives and about childhood. They agree that Ma likely left to escape Pa's abuse. Kya talks about Tate, and Jodie encourages Kya to forgive Tate and have a relationship with him.

Chapter 34 takes place in 1969. Jackson and Purdue arrive at Kya's home in the marsh. She is not there. They search the shack, and they find a red hat. Fibers from the hat are identical to the fibers from the crime scene. Chapter 35 takes place in July of 1969. Kya thinks about Tate and considers Jodie's suggestion that if Kya loves Tate, Kya should give Tate another chance.

CHAPTER 36-40

Chapter 36 takes place in 1969. Jackson and Purdue consider Kya's possible motive, but they are unconvinced that being jilted by Chase is enough of a motive for an arrest. However, after a man named Rodney speaks with them, they decide that they have enough of a motive for an arrest. (The narrative does not yet reveal what information Rodney conveyed.) In Chapter 37, it is December, 1969. Jackson and Purdue ambush Kya while she is in her boat and arrest her. Chapter 38 takes place in 1970. Kya is on trial for murder, and if she is convicted, she may receive the death penalty.

The materialization of Kya's successful career as a naturalist stands as further sign of her personal capabilities and worth, and thus the novel further demonstrates how the townspeople's antipathy and prejudice towards Kya was unwarranted and unjust. Even before the publication of Kya's book, the novel demonstrates Kya as a kind and capable person, despite the fears of the townspeople. Kya is able to live on her own in the swamp, and despite the ridicule and persecution of the townspeople, she has proven herself capable of love and loyalty. Moreover, her self-teachings have demonstrated her own profound capacity for learning and hard work.

Kya is so dedicated in her love of nature and her study/exploration of it that she is able to begin a career as a naturalist in her early twenties, despite having no formal schooling. Tate even says, after reading her book, "Kya, your book is a wonder." Kya's career success is not a necessary component of proving that she is a valuable person and deserves dignity. However, her success does help to work against the townspeople's false, unfair, prejudicial notions of her as a feral, subhuman entity.

The reappearance of Jodie helps Kya process her past and the import of her family connections, and Kya's forgiveness of Jodie demonstrates how interpersonal redemption can be claimed even after abandonment years of separation. Jodie seeks out Kya after he sees her book in a store, and he asks for forgiveness for abandoning Kya. Kya forgives him and seems delighted to be reunited with her brother. She is then saddened to learn of her mother's death. Kya says, "I've had no family, no news of family for most of my life. Now within a few minutes I've found a brother and lost my mother."

Although this moment is □uite tragic, it also reaffirms the value of family connections in Kya's eyes, for she is glad to be reunited with Jodie, and she feels the immense loss of her mother's death. Moreover, with Jodie present, Kya finally has someone with whom to discuss the salient events of her childhood, such as Pa's abuse of the family and Ma's eventual departure. Although it is painful to dredge up these memories, it seems to be a therapeutic process for Kya, allowing her to come to more direct terms with the difficult and emotionally scarring aspects of her childhood.

As difficulties mount for Kya, Tate still functions as a potential source for hope and love, and the narrative seems to position Kya and Tate's relationship as a central hope for true and lasting happiness in Kya's life. After Kya tells Jodie about Kya and Tate's history, Jodie encourages Kya to give Tate another chance. Jodie says, "Let's face it, a lot of times love doesn't work out. Yet even when it fails, it connects you to others and, in the end, that's all you have, the connections." Jodie says that because Tate recognized his folly, and because love still seems to exist between Kya and Tate, then Kya should give her relationship with Tate another chance. Thus, even as Kya must face her criminal trial, Tate seems to represent the possibility of hope.

Chapter 39 takes place in August of 1969. Chase visits Kya in the marsh. He says that he wants to resume his relationship with her. When Kya refuses, Chase hits Kya and tries to rape her. Kya hits him in the testicles and runs away. She notices two men in a boat who witnessed the struggle. Chapter 40 takes place in 1970. The prosecutor calls to the stand Rodney Horn, one of the two men who witnessed the struggle. Rodney states what he saw. When the defense attorney cross-examines, he has Rodney reiterate the fact that Chase was trying to rape Kya and that Kya was defending herself.

CHAPTER 41-45

Chapter 41 takes place in August, 1969. Kya fears retaliation from Chase, and she knows that the townspeople and police will not help her, as Chase is a popular member of the community, and she is an outcast. Chapter 42 takes place in 1970. Kya is in a jail cell between trial sessions. She helps calm herself by reciting poetry to herself.

Chapter 43 takes place in September, 1969. Kya receives an invitation from her publisher to meet with him in Greenville. Tate visits Kya and notices the bruise on Kya's face inflicted by Chase. Kya does not tell Tate about the attempted rape. In the following days, Kya lives in fear of Chase and tries to figure out what she should do. Chapter 44 takes place in 1970. Before the trial, the prosecution offers a plea bargain for limited jail time, but Kya chooses to go to trial. Later, Tate visits Kya in the jail to comfort her.

Chapter 45 takes place in 1970. The trial continues. The prosecution calls the county coroner as a witness. The coroner affirms evidence, such as the red fibers, that supports the conclusion that Kya may have killed Chase by pushing him through the trapdoor in the fire tower. However, the defense attorney then cross-examines, and the coroner affirms that the evidence is circumstantial, that there is no conclusive evidence, and that the red fibers may have been transferred to Chase at any time during his relationship with Kya.

CHAPTER 46-50

Chapter 46 takes place in September of 1969. Jumpin' notices the bruise on Kya's face. Kya makes Jumpin' promise not to tell anyone that Chase attacked her, as she knows that everyone will side with Chase and further persecute her. Jumpin' agrees not to tell anyone. Chapter 47 takes place in 1970. The trial continues. The prosecution calls Sheriff Jackson as a witness. On the witness stand, Jackson talks about the suspicious lack of footprints and fingerprints at the crime scene. During cross-examination, Jackson admits that it is possible that Chase fell by accident and that the fire tower was a safety hazard.

In Chapter 48, Kya leaves for Greenville in late October, 1969, and she returns two days later. When she returns, Jumpin' tells her that Chase was found dead. In Chapter 49, during the trial, the defense attorney □uestions bus drivers who say that they are do not remember seeing Kya on any bused on the night of Chase's death.

As the novel progresses, the narrative maintains a careful balance of uncertainty regarding Kya's guilt or innocence, thereby maintaining both intrigue and momentum in the story. As the mystery and procedural elements of the book begin to take focus, the narrative takes on more emphasized elements of the mystery and thriller genre. Moreover, the narrative deftly gives alternating evidence for and against Kya's guilt so as to keep the reader engrossed and uncertain. For example, this dynamic can be viewed in the procedural elements of the courtroom scenes, as the prosecution interviews witnesses and then allows the defense to cross-examine them in accordance with standard legal procedure.

With each witness, the prosecution builds evidence seemingly in support of Kya's guilt, and then the defense demonstrates how none of the evidence is conclusive. For example, the coroner states that "the evidence would support that conclusion" that Chase was murdered. However, during cross-examination, the defense attorney demonstrates that just because evidence possibly supports a conclusion does not make the evidence conclusive. Another example is when Jackson is on the witness stand. He emanates a belief that Kya is definitely guilty, but during cross-examination, he must admit that it is possible that Chase fell accidentally.

As the narrative develops Kya's possible motive for killing Chase, the narrative does not necessarily assert that Chase deserved to die, but the story does examine the possible correlation between Chase's horrific actions and Kya's sense of fear. When Chase attempts to rape Kya, the full depth of corruption in his character is revealed. Chase not only lies to and manipulates women, but his sense of entitlement apparently can drive him to violent actions such as attempting rape. This attack leads Kya to a state of profound fear. The narration states, "Chase would not let this go. Being isolated was one thing; living in fear, quite another."

This narration dynamic can also be read as carrying specifically feminist themes, for Kya has no recourse against her attacker in part due to male privilege and prejudice against women. This narrative dynamic functions to simulate the sense of helplessness that women often face in instances of sexual assault, as sexism and prejudice often weight recourse against the victim.

Kya's position of helplessness not only demonstrates dynamics of sexism, but it is also shaped by the dynamics of prejudice that the novel has explored since very early in the story. As the narrative has shown, the townspeople view Kya as an outcast. In contrast, the townspeople view Chase not only as one of their own, but also as one of their most beloved members. As Kya says to Jumpin', "You know how it is. They'll take his side. They'll say I'm just stirring up trouble…It would end in big trouble [for me]." Jumpin' and Tate, both realizing that Kya is correct in this assessment, agree not to tell anyone about Chase's attack on Kya.

In this way, the novel demonstrates how privilege can shield a person from proper justice for wrongdoings. Thus, if Kya did kill Chase, the murder would likely have been motivated by this realization that there was no other recourse by which to secure her own safety.

Chapter 50 takes place in 1970. The prosecution calls Patti Love to the stand. She gives testimony about the shell necklace that Chase always wore, which was a gift from Kya and which was not found on his body. The prosecution presents a painting that Kya made and gave to Chase. The painting depicts Kya and Chase in the fire tower together.

CHAPTER 51-55

In Chapter 51, the prosecution calls a fisherman to the stand. The fisherman testifies that he saw Kya on her boat heading towards the fire tower on the night of Chase's death. However, during cross-examination, the fisherman says that he cannot state with full certainty that it was definitely Kya that he saw. In Chapter 52, the defense calls to the stand a woman who saw Kya board a bus to Greenville on the afternoon of October 28, 1969. The defense then calls the owner of the Greenville motel where Kya stayed. The owner says that he never saw Kya leave her room on the night of Chase's death. However, on cross-examination, he admits that she could have slipped out without him noticing.

In Chapter 53, the prosecution and defense each give their closing arguments. In his closing argument, the defense attorney emphasizes the lack of conclusive evidence. He also emphasizes the fact that Kya has been unfairly persecuted as an outcast for her entire life, and he frames the trial itself as a symptom of that persecution. In Chapter 54, the jury deliberates and reaches a verdict: not guilty. Many spectators in the courtroom are disappointed by the verdict. Kya is deeply relieved. In Chapter 55, Jodie brings Kya back to her home in the marsh and implores her not to give up on humanity, despite all of the trauma she has experienced.

Kya considers his advice but reaches no conclusions. Later, she sees the sheriff and Tate, and it looks like the sheriff is taking Tate into custody.

CHAPTER 56-57

Chapter 56, Kya and the reader learn that the sheriff was merely informing Tate that his father had died. Tate mourns at his father's grave and then goes to Kya. They declare their everlasting love for each other.

In Chapter 57, Tate proposes marriage to Kya. Kya rejects the idea of formal marriage and says that they are already married. Tate moves in with Kya in her home in the marsh. Kya never goes into town again, but she continues writing her books. As time passes, community sentiment changes in favor of Kya, and people agree that she never should have been arrested. One day, Jumpin' dies, and Kya mourns him, as he was like a father to her. Over the years Kya continues her work, and Tate sets up his own lab in his and Kya's home. They try to have children, but they unfortunately are never successful in doing so.

Kya dies at the age of 64. Tate then goes through her belongings and discovers that the local poet, Amanda Hamilton, was actually Kya, writing under a pseudonym. He also finds the shell necklace that Kya gave to Chase. Tate realizes that Kya really did kill Chase. Tate throws the necklace into the water so that no one will ever find it.

The defense attorney's closing arguments help to thematically emphasize the nature of persecution and antipathy, both towards Kya and in general, for the attorney encourages both the reader and the jury to see how the trial is symptomatic of that persecution. The defense attorney not only points out the lack of conclusive evidence to convict Kya, but he also frames the trial as a moral failing in itself. As the reader knows, Kya has been the victim of general persecution for her entire life, as other people see her as an outcast despite her kindness, sensitivity, and intelligence. The defense attorney closes his arguments by stating, "It is time, at last, for us to be fair to the Marsh Girl."

Despite the fact that, as the reader later learns, Kya really did kill Chase, the defense attorney is essentially correct in his assessment. Kya was arrested without conclusive evidence, largely due to the unjust prejudices against her. This dynamic demonstrates the degree to which prejudice can overturn principles of decency and morality. Moreover, the mental and emotional toll of such prejudice weighs heavily on Kya, for when Jodie encourages her not to give up on humanity, she is not ready to so right away.

The saga of Kya and Tate's life following the trial seems to reaffirm Kya's general decency and personal worth, and while Kya is not free of moral imperfection, the novel presents the possibility that persecution and injustice were the true roots of evil in the narrative. In the years following the trial, Kya and Tate are able to have a fulfilling life together as loving partners. They live together in the swamp and lead productive lives, contributing to scientific knowledge. In addition, although Kya does not become a part of the surrounding community, the townspeople look more kindly on her: "As time passed, most everyone agreed the sheriff never should've arrested her. After all, there was no hard evidence against her, no real proof of a crime. It had been truly cruel to treat a shy, natural creature that way."

A reader may argue that because Kya really did kill Chase, she is not morally justified in any way. However, one may also argue that Kya had no choice, as it was her only recourse to defend herself, and that those non-ideal moral conditions were created by the atmosphere of persecution that surrounded her.

At the end of the novel, Tate and the reader learn that Kya really did kill Chase, and this revelation forces the reader to confront the moral tensions created between the inherent immorality of murder and the factors that drove Kya to the act. Killing Chase appears to have been the only immoral act that Kya ever committed in her life, and she felt that she had no choice but to kill Chase in order to protect herself, both from Chase and from further persecution by the community. On one hand, a reader may argue that the fact of Kya's guilt overrides all other moral considerations and that she should have been arrested and convicted for the crime.

On the other hand, the arrest and trial itself were technically bourne on motivations of prejudice in place of conclusive evidence, and additionally, Kya had no other means by which to protect herself. The narrative seems to leave this moral question open-ended for the reader's consideration, but the dynamics of persecution that functioned against Kya still remain thematically relevant in portraying the immorality of unjust persecution.

QUESTIONS

What happens when Kya attends school?   (from Prologue – Chapter 6)

    A. The teacher hits her.
    B. The students make fun of her.
    C. A student steals Kya's shoes.
    D. Kya falls into a puddle.

2. How does Tate react after reading Kya's first book?
    (from Chapters 30 – 38)

    A. He becomes jealous of Kya.
    B. He says that the book is great.
    C. He says that the book is not very good.
    D. He is indifferent.

3. What does Pa say about his family history?   (from Chapters 7 – 16)

    A. He says that his family was always poor.
    B. He says that his family used to be wealthy.
    C. He says that his ancestors were knights.
    D. He says that he is the illegitimate son of a politician.

4. How does Kya's trial end?   (from Chapters 50 – 57)

    A. The jury is unable to reach a verdict.
    B. The jury finds Kya guilty.
    C. The jury finds Kya not guilty.
    D. The judge calls a mistrial.

5. Where do Kya and Chase first have sex? (from Chapters 23 – 29)

    A. At Chase's house.
    B. A motel.
    C. In Kya's shack.
    D. In the river.

ANSWERS

1. A
2. B
3. A
4. C
5. B

CONCLUSION

The novel's main narrative opens in the marshland near the fictional town of Barkley Cove, North Carolina. Seven-year-old Catherine "Kya" Clark lives in a shack in the swamp with her mother, father, and siblings. However, one day, Kya's mother leaves the shack forever in order to escape the physical abuse inflicted by Kya's father. Kya's siblings soon leave on their own as well, leaving only Kya and Pa. Pa spends increasingly more time away from the shack over the years, and when Kya is about ten years old, Pa leaves forever. Kya has become thoroughly self-sufficient by this time, living off the land and occasionally trading in town for necessary supplies.

When Kya is 14 years old, a kind local boy named Tate Walker begins to visit her, and he teaches her how to read. He is about four years older than Kya. He also gives Kya his old textbooks from school. When Kya is 15 years old, she and Tate fall in love, but Tate insists that they do not have sex until Kya is older. Tate soon leaves for college, and although he promises to love and remember Kya, Kya feels abandoned. When Kya is 19 years old, she becomes attracted to a young local man named Chase Andrews. Chase begins visiting her often. Chase says that he loves her and is eager to have sex with her. Kya refuses at first, but after about a year, she consents.

Tate eventually returns to Barkley Cove in order to perform scientific research on the marshland. He visits Kya and asks for forgiveness, but she refuses to take him back. Tate sees that Kya has performed much of her own research on the marshland, and he urges Kya to submit it to publishers. Tate also warns Kya that Chase is a dishonest womanizer. One day, Kya sees in the newspaper that Chase has become engaged to someone else. She is heartbroken.

Later, she submits her research to publishers, and when she is 22 years old, a book of her research is published under her name. Kya's brother Jodie sees the book in a store and returns to the swamp to reconnect with Kya. Jodie encourages Kya to give Tate another chance.

Chase eventually visits Kya and says that he wants to continue his relationship with her, despite the fact that he is married to someone else. When Kya refuses him, Chase tries to rape her. She hits him and escapes. Kya realizes that because Chase is such a popular member of the town, and because she is an outcast for living in the swamp, she has no recourse. One day, in October of 1969, Chase's body is found near the swamp. He appears to have fallen—or possibly have been pushed—out of a fire watchtower. The sheriff investigates and arrests Kya.

However, the evidence is inconclusive and circumstantial, and Kya is acquitted. She and Tate declare their love for each other, and they live together in the swamp. Kya continues her career as a naturalist, and Tate continues his career as a researcher. Kya dies at age 64, after which Tate finds evidence that seems to prove that

Kya killed Chase. He disposes of the evidence so that no one will ever find it.

Thank You, and more...

Thank you for spending your time to read this book, I hope now you hold a greater knowledge about ***Where the Crawdad Sings.***

Before you go, would you mind leaving us a review on where you purchased your book?

It will mean a lot to us and help us continue making more summaries for you and for others.

Thank you once again!

Yours warmly,

FURTHER READINGS

Here are some other great book's summary

(Just click on it)

1- Summary of Educated: A Memoir by Tara Westover

https://www.amazon.com/dp/B07NXWHK7Q/

2- Summary of Building a StoryBrand by Donald Miller

https://www.amazon.com/dp/B07P1XPTZF/

3- Summary of The Culture Code by Daniel Coyle

https://www.amazon.com/dp/B07P9PRGQT/